MAYER SMITH

Love's Tidal Magic

This book was professionally typeset on Reedsy.
Find out more at reedsy.com

Contents

One

The Storm's First Whisper

The wind came first, a soft murmur against the windowpane that grew into an insistent howl. Lila stood at the edge of the cliffs, eyes fixed on the horizon, watching the storm gather in the distance like an angry, darkened mass. The sea was restless, its waves lashing against the jagged rocks below, each crash louder than the last. She could taste the salt in the air, feel it cling to her lips, her skin, the ocean's rhythm pulsing through the air like the beat of a heart.

Her fingers curled around the railing, knuckles pale, and for a moment, she allowed herself to sink into the quiet before the chaos. The storm had been building for days, each gust of wind a harbinger of something more, something… unnatural. It wasn't just the weather that unsettled her; it was something in the town itself, the way it seemed to hold its breath.

The people here were waiting for something. Or someone.

Turning away from the sea, Lila made her way to the old wooden door of the study, her boots tapping softly on the floorboards. She hesitated before entering, as if the very air within the room held the weight of unspoken words. The door creaked as she pushed it open, revealing the disarray inside—the scattered papers on the desk, the half-empty mug of cold coffee, the faint smell of seaweed and dust that clung to the room like a second skin.

"You're late," came the voice from the corner, low and gravelly.

Lila's pulse quickened at the sound of it, and she glanced over her shoulder, meeting the gaze of Kai, leaning against the wall with his arms crossed. His dark eyes, almost black in the dim light, held hers with an intensity that made her heart stutter. The storm outside seemed to echo in the rawness of his gaze, in the tension that thrummed beneath the surface of his words.

"I didn't realize there was a schedule for this," she replied, her voice sharper than she intended.

Kai's lips twitched into a half-smile, but it didn't reach his eyes. "The research waits for no one, Lila."

She couldn't argue with that. The strange phenomenon in the waters had brought her back to this forsaken place, and now, she was ensnared by it—by the mystery of it, by the allure of something she couldn't quite grasp. Something dangerous.

"I'm here now," she said, pushing past the knot in her throat. She moved toward the desk, her gaze flitting over the array of maps, weather reports, and scattered notes. "Has there been any progress?"

Kai's posture stiffened. He was always so guarded, always so distant. There were times, brief moments, when she thought she saw something deeper in him—something far more complicated than the rugged fisherman who stood before her. But those moments were fleeting, vanishing like shadows as soon as she reached for them.

"You could say that," he muttered. "The water's acting strange, even for here."

Lila nodded, her fingers trailing over the edge of one of the maps. There was something about this town—something hidden beneath the surface that didn't sit right with her. But there was no time to dwell on that. The storm was coming, and the waters were rising. Every day, they seemed to grow more erratic, more dangerous. The townspeople were whispering about it again—about the curse, about the magic that pulsed beneath the waves. But no one would speak of it openly. Fear had kept its grip on this place for far too long.

The room seemed to close in on her, the walls thick with secrets she wasn't ready to uncover.

"You didn't answer my question," she said, her voice a little tighter than she meant. "What's happening with the tides?"

Kai didn't answer immediately. Instead, he stood up straighter, eyes narrowing slightly as he watched her, as though he were trying to gauge her reaction to something unsaid. His eyes, dark like the storm itself, flickered to the map. His gaze lingered, but for a moment, it was almost as if he were looking through her, not at her.

"I've been keeping track," he said finally, his voice quiet but steady. "The tides aren't just erratic. They're… changing. And not in any natural way."

Lila's brow furrowed as she stepped closer. "What do you mean?"

"There are patterns," he continued, his tone low and measured. "They're shifting in ways that shouldn't be possible. The currents, the temperature, even the way the seaweed is growing… everything's different."

The room felt colder now, the shadows longer, stretching across the walls. Lila felt the weight of those words, heavy and suffocating. Something was happening here, something that no one understood, something that had been buried for years beneath the tide. And she had no choice but to dig into it, to uncover it—because if she didn't, the people she loved would pay the price.

She met Kai's eyes again. There was an unspoken understanding between them, something raw and undeniable. The town, the storm, the sea… they were all tangled up in the same thing.

"What else haven't you told me?" she asked, her voice barely above a whisper.

Kai's jaw clenched, and for a moment, he looked like he might walk away, but then something flickered in his eyes, and he stepped toward her, his voice low and dangerous. "You don't know what you're asking for."

She swallowed hard. "I need to know, Kai."

For a heartbeat, the room was silent, save for the distant rumble of thunder outside. Then, slowly, Kai reached into his pocket and pulled out a weathered, leather-bound notebook. He slid it across the desk toward her.

"Take a look," he said, his voice hard. "But don't say I didn't warn you."

Lila hesitated before she opened it, her fingers brushing over the old pages. The ink was faded in places, the handwriting almost indecipherable, but she could make out enough. There were notes, diagrams, and maps—many of them centered on the sea, on the tides, on something ancient that lurked beneath the surface. Her pulse quickened as she read through the words, realizing that the danger she had come to study was far greater than she had anticipated.

There was a curse. A pact made long ago with the sea. And somewhere, buried in these pages, was the key to breaking it—or dying trying.

Lila slammed the book shut, her heart racing. "Kai—"

But before she could finish, the wind outside howled louder, rattling the windows. The storm was closer now, the air thick with anticipation, as though the world was holding its breath.

Kai's expression softened for just a moment, and for the first time since she'd met him, Lila saw something like fear in his eyes. Not for himself. For her.

"You're not ready for this," he whispered, his voice barely audible over the storm.

Lila swallowed the lump in her throat, steeling herself. "I'll be ready," she said, her voice steady, even though her hands trembled as she picked up the notebook. "You can't keep hiding from this. From whatever it is."

Kai didn't answer. He didn't need to. The storm outside was already speaking louder than words ever could.

Two

Echoes of the Depths

The morning after the storm arrived with a bruised sky, gray and swollen, as if the heavens were still recovering from the fury of the night. Lila stood on the deck of the research vessel, her eyes scanning the horizon where the sea seemed to stretch into eternity, a jagged line of white foam marking the churning waters below. The wind had died down, but the air was thick with a heavy, unnatural stillness that clung to her skin like a warning.

The ocean's vastness was both a comfort and a threat. It whispered secrets to those who dared listen—secrets she hadn't yet uncovered.

The scent of salt lingered in the air, sharp and pungent, but there was something else, something sweeter, as though the ocean was teasing her with the promise of something hidden beneath the surface. Her fingers brushed the railing, and she felt a shiver travel up her spine. The sea felt alive today, alive in a way that sent unease skittering along her nerves.

"You're staring at it like it might speak to you," Kai's voice cut through the silence, rough and low, as if it had been waiting to break the tension.

Lila turned, surprised to see him standing at the entrance to the cabin, the early morning light casting a halo around his silhouette. His tousled hair was damp from the dew that clung to the ship's weathered wood, and the dark circles beneath his eyes only added to the raw intensity that always seemed to cling to him. He was different today—tenser, sharper. She could feel it in the air between them.

"I think it might," she replied, her voice more confident than she felt. She pushed a strand of hair behind her ear, her gaze flickering back to the sea. "It's not the storm I'm worried about. It's the aftermath."

Kai stepped closer, his boots creaking on the old wood, his presence like a weight that seemed to draw her in, without even trying. "You're still looking for answers, aren't you?"

She nodded, the taste of salt on her tongue, and the oppressive weight of the mystery settling over her like a fog. "I can feel it, Kai. There's something off about the water—something I can't explain. I need to know what's causing it."

The wind shifted, tugging at her jacket, and the faintest whisper of a laugh escaped Kai's lips, low and rough. "You always did have a stubborn streak," he said, his voice oddly tender as he moved closer, standing just a breath away from her. "But you're playing with fire, Lila. The deeper you go, the harder it'll be to get out. And I'm not sure you'll even want to."

Lila turned her head slightly, her gaze meeting his, and for a moment, the world around them seemed to disappear. His words hovered in the air like a dangerous promise, the tension between them so thick it could be cut with a knife. But she didn't look away. She couldn't.

"Maybe I don't want to," she murmured, a breathless truth escaping her lips before she could stop it.

Kai's lips twitched, his eyes darkening, but he didn't respond immediately. Instead, he turned his gaze back to the sea, his jaw tightening. "I've seen what happens when people dig too deep into this town's history. Into what's buried beneath the water."

She watched him closely, sensing that there was more he wasn't telling her. More than he was willing to admit. The vulnerability in his voice—a crack she hadn't expected—was a rarity, and Lila felt an unfamiliar pull in her chest, a mixture of pity and something darker, more dangerous. But before she could press him for more, he spoke again, his tone colder this time.

"Let's get to work," he said, a clear dismissal.

They moved inside the small cabin, the door creaking shut

behind them, and the familiar scent of damp wood and coffee filled the air. Lila dropped her jacket on the chair and made her way to the table, where the research notes were spread out like a map to a secret world. The vessel rocked gently beneath their feet, the water lapping against the hull, and the rhythmic motion seemed to pulse in time with her own anxious heartbeat.

She tried to focus, tried to push aside the discomfort that had settled deep in her bones, but every glance toward Kai only seemed to pull her in deeper. His presence was magnetic, like the pull of the tides themselves—compelling, relentless, and dangerous. She could feel the weight of his gaze on her, as though he were constantly watching, always waiting for her to slip.

But slip she would not.

Her fingers trembled slightly as she opened the notebook again, her eyes scanning the faded ink, trying to make sense of the fragmented notes. The diagrams seemed to make sense, the patterns in the tides and currents, but it was the map that caught her eye—the one marked with crosses and circled areas deep in the heart of the sea. The place that no one spoke of. The place where the sea seemed to hold its breath.

"What's this?" she asked, pointing to the map, her voice tight.

Kai didn't look up. He didn't need to; he already knew what she was asking. He sighed, the sound heavy with years of buried regret, and his hands clenched around the edge of the counter.

"Where the sea refuses to let go," he said quietly, his voice rough, the words almost a whisper.

Lila's breath caught in her throat. There was something in his voice—a thread of something dark, something he wasn't ready to confront. Something ancient.

"This is where it started," he continued, his eyes flickering to hers, almost apologetic. "The pact. The curse. Everything that's wrong with this place."

She stared at him, trying to find the man behind the walls he so carefully constructed. The mystery of the sea was one thing; the enigma of Kai was another. But they were tangled together, weren't they? The deeper she dug into one, the more she uncovered the other.

"Tell me about it," she said, her voice soft, coaxing him, pulling him closer with each word.

For a moment, he hesitated, his gaze flickering to the window as though the storm might return with its fury, as if the words themselves could summon it. He swallowed hard and turned away, moving to the window as if seeking refuge in the view.

"I can't," he said, his voice strained. "Not yet."

The knot in Lila's stomach tightened, a flare of frustration igniting in her chest. She could feel the edge of something dark and forbidden just out of reach, and it gnawed at her. But she held her tongue, instead turning back to the map, trying to piece together the fragments.

There had to be something she could use. Some clue, some key that would unlock the mystery.

Suddenly, there was a loud crack, a sharp, thunderous sound from the depths of the sea. The ship shuddered beneath their feet, the glass rattling in the windows. Lila's heart skipped a beat, her gaze snapping to the window as the ocean seemed to roar with fury.

"What the hell was that?" she demanded, her voice high with shock.

Kai didn't answer immediately. Instead, he moved to the helm, his face set in grim determination.

"It's starting," he said quietly, barely above a whisper.

Lila's pulse raced as she grabbed her jacket and followed him onto the deck, the wind biting at her skin, the ocean raging with a newfound intensity. Waves taller than buildings crashed against the hull, and the air was thick with the scent of something unnatural.

In the distance, the sea seemed to darken, and the horizon twisted in on itself, a perfect storm gathering with a force that felt far beyond nature.

Kai's voice broke through the chaos. "We need to leave. Now."

But it was too late.

Lila could feel it. The pulse of the sea, the pulse of something far older and far darker than either of them had ever known.

And it was calling to her.

Three

Shifting Tides

The dawn was broken by the eerie calm of the sea, the once-chaotic waters now lying still, as though holding their breath. Lila sat in the small cabin, her hands trembling as she sipped the warm, bitter coffee Kai had made. It was a ritual of sorts now, the way he would silently make the coffee and leave it for her, a gesture both simple and loaded with a depth she couldn't quite understand. The steam rose from the mug in wisps, curling through the stale air, but it did nothing to soothe the unsettled feeling gnawing at her chest.

She didn't know what it was about this place, this town, that left her constantly on edge. Was it the storm? The secret buried in the sea? Or was it the quiet intensity of Kai, who seemed to carry a storm of his own within him?

Lila's eyes flickered toward the map again, still spread out on the table in front of her. There was a new urgency in her thoughts as she traced her finger over the red X marking the location they'd discussed yesterday—the heart of the storm, the place where the sea refused to let go. She didn't know why, but something about it felt… wrong. The air around her thickened with the weight of untold stories.

But it wasn't just the map that unsettled her. It was Kai, standing by the window, his eyes distant and focused on the horizon, his body rigid as if every muscle was taut with anticipation. She could feel the energy building between them, an unspoken tension that seemed to crackle in the air, the silence charged with meaning.

The door creaked open behind her, and she didn't need to turn to know it was him. She felt the room shift as he stepped inside, the air thick with his presence.

"We need to talk," his voice came, low and gravelly, cutting through the stillness.

Lila looked up, her heart hammering in her chest. There was something different about him today. His usual stoic demeanor was gone, replaced with something that felt more fragile, more raw. She could see it in the set of his jaw, the way his shoulders were hunched as though carrying a weight too heavy to bear.

"About what?" Lila asked, her voice steady, even as a storm brewed inside her.

He hesitated for a long moment, his gaze flickering to the map, then back to her, before finally speaking.

"About what we're really dealing with here."

Lila's pulse quickened, and she set her mug down, the soft clink of porcelain against wood cutting through the tension. She leaned forward, her eyes fixed on his. "Kai, you've been holding back. What aren't you telling me?"

He took a step closer, and the room seemed to shrink, the space between them closing with every movement he made. She could feel the heat radiating from him, a warmth that did nothing to calm the chill running through her veins. His eyes, dark and unreadable, locked with hers, and for a moment, she felt as though he was trying to decide whether or not to trust her.

"You wouldn't believe me," he said softly, his voice barely above a whisper, yet heavy with meaning. "You don't want to know what's really out there."

Lila shook her head, refusing to back down. "Try me."

The corner of his mouth twitched, almost as though he were amused by her persistence, but it quickly disappeared, replaced by a mask of stoicism. He moved toward the desk, running a hand through his dark hair, his fingers trembling just slightly.

"Do you believe in curses, Lila?" His voice was hoarse, as if the question itself burned in his throat.

She frowned. "Not in the way you mean."

Kai let out a low, bitter laugh. "You should. This town, this sea… it's all tied to something ancient. Something we can't undo."

Lila stood up now, moving closer to him, her eyes never leaving his face. "Then tell me. What's happening? Why is the sea reacting like this? Why are the tides changing?"

His eyes darted to the map, the one that marked the mysterious spot, and then back to her. His expression hardened, and she could see the struggle in his gaze—the battle between what he knew and what he was willing to share.

"Because of the pact," he said, his voice low, almost lost in the weight of his own words. "It was made centuries ago, by the people who settled here. They bargained with the sea, thinking they could control it, but all they did was anger it. Now it's fighting back, in ways we can't begin to understand. And you're too close to it, Lila. You don't know what you're getting yourself into."

Lila's breath caught in her throat as she processed his words. She had heard the rumors, of course—whispers about the town's dark history, about the strange things that happened when the sea grew restless. But she had never truly believed them, not until now.

"You're telling me the sea is… cursed?" Her voice trembled, though she tried to hide it.

Kai nodded, his expression dark. "It's not just the sea, Lila. It's everything here. This town… it's built on the bones of the past, and those bones are starting to rise again."

A shiver ran down her spine at his words, and she fought the urge to step back, to flee from the weight of the truth he was offering her. But she couldn't. She had to know, had to understand what had brought her here, what the sea wanted from her.

"What do you want me to do, Kai?" she asked, her voice soft, uncertain.

He looked at her then, really looked at her, and for the first time since they had met, she saw something in his eyes that she hadn't expected—fear. It was fleeting, quickly masked by the walls he had so carefully built, but it was there, and it unsettled her more than anything else.

"You need to leave," he said, his voice rough. "Before it's too late."

Lila shook her head, her chest tightening. "I can't. Not now. Not when I'm this close."

Kai's eyes darkened, his gaze flicking toward the window as if he were searching for something on the horizon, something he was too afraid to confront. The wind outside picked up again, and Lila could feel the tension in the air, thickening, charging the space between them. She took a step closer, determined not to let him shut her out.

"Please," she whispered, her voice breaking through the silence. "Tell me everything. I can't leave without understanding what's really at stake."

For a long moment, he didn't answer. The storm outside seemed to answer for him, its winds howling against the hull of the ship, the sea rising in response to something unseen, something far older than either of them. Finally, Kai turned to face her, his jaw clenched, his expression hard.

"I'm not trying to protect you, Lila," he said, his voice dark and filled with a depth of emotion she wasn't ready to understand. "I'm trying to save you."

But his words felt like a warning, one that she couldn't ignore. The ocean was calling to her, and no matter how hard she tried to resist, she knew it wouldn't let her go.

"Then help me," she whispered, the plea slipping from her lips before she could stop it. "Please."

Kai's eyes softened for a brief moment, but it was fleeting. He turned away, his back to her as he gazed out at the darkening waters.

"You're already too far gone," he muttered, more to himself than to her.

And as the last light of day began to fade, Lila realized with chilling clarity that she was in deeper than she ever imagined—and there would be no turning back.

Four

Tangled Hearts and Secrets

The rain came in waves, battering the research vessel with relentless intensity, as if the sky itself were mourning what the sea had long concealed. Lila stood in the galley, watching the droplets race each other down the glass, her breath fogging the cold surface as she stared out into the gloom. The ocean stretched before her, infinite and impossible to understand, its waves violent and unforgiving in their ceaseless rhythm. Yet, beneath the tumultuous waters, she felt the stirrings of something ancient, something dark. It had been growing steadily since she first set foot in this cursed town, and now, as the storm roared outside, it felt more alive than ever.

Kai had been distant since their conversation the day before. He avoided her eyes, spoke only when necessary, and disappeared into the bowels of the ship when she tried to approach him. His silence weighed heavily on her, and despite the storm's fury, she felt a pressing need to reach him. To break through the walls he'd so carefully built around himself. But every time she tried, he slipped further away.

The creaking of the door interrupted her thoughts, and she turned to find him standing in the doorway, soaked through from the rain, his hair dripping in rivulets down his neck. His eyes were shadowed, but the storm outside was nothing compared to the storm raging within him.

"You shouldn't be standing here," Kai said, his voice hoarse from the wind. His gaze briefly flickered to hers before he stepped forward, his wet boots leaving dark marks on the wooden floor. "It's too dangerous."

Lila couldn't help but notice the sharp edge to his voice, the hardness that had crept into his every word since the moment they'd started this journey together. It was as though the weight of everything he knew was pushing him further away, even as she felt herself being drawn in.

"I'm not afraid of the storm," she said quietly, her eyes locking with his. "But I am afraid of what's happening. What you're not telling me."

Kai's jaw clenched, the muscles in his face tightening as though he were holding back something, something powerful and painful. He didn't look at her for a long moment, as if searching for the right words, or perhaps the courage to speak them.

"You think you want the truth, Lila," he said finally, his voice a gravelly whisper, "but you don't. Not about this place. Not about what's in the water."

She stepped closer, the space between them narrowing. "I don't care what it costs. I need to understand. Whatever this is, whatever's happening—it's not just about the sea anymore, is it?"

Kai's eyes softened for the briefest of moments, but it was quickly replaced with something darker, something that chilled her to her bones. He reached out and placed a hand on her shoulder, a touch that was both gentle and possessive, as though he were holding her in place against a force greater than them both.

"It's not just the sea," he murmured, his voice barely audible. "It's the town, the people. There are things here that you won't be able to walk away from once you know them."

Lila felt a cold wave of realization wash over her, but before she could speak, the ship lurched violently, throwing her off balance. She caught herself against the wall, her pulse spiking in sudden fear. The wind howled outside, and the rain hit the windows like a thousand tiny fists, each drop a promise of something coming—something unstoppable. Kai was already by her side, his hands firm as he steadied her.

"Get below deck," he ordered, his voice suddenly urgent.

"I'm not leaving you alone," Lila said, her heart pounding in her chest. The connection between them, fragile as it was, deepened with every passing moment. The intensity between them, the unspoken pull that had been there since their first meeting, was becoming too powerful to ignore.

Kai turned to face her, his expression hard, his lips pressed into a thin line. "You don't get it, Lila. I'm not the one who's in danger here. It's you."

Her breath caught in her throat at the finality in his tone. There was a desperation in his eyes, a fear that echoed in his voice. But she didn't move. Instead, she stepped closer, her gaze unyielding.

"I'm not leaving," she whispered, her voice barely audible over the roar of the storm. "Not now. Not when I'm so close."

For a moment, he just stood there, watching her, as if trying to read her, trying to make sense of the stubborn woman who refused to walk away. His eyes were dark, impossibly intense, and in them, Lila saw something she hadn't expected— vulnerability. The kind of vulnerability that came with knowing too much, with carrying a burden so heavy that it could crush a person's soul.

"You don't know what you're asking," he said finally, his voice rough with something unspoken. "This isn't just about breaking a curse, Lila. It's about survival. And I won't let you be a part of this… not if it means losing you."

The words hit her like a physical blow, and for a moment, she felt as though the floor had been swept out from beneath her. She knew the truth in his words, felt the gravity of them deep in her gut. But still, she couldn't walk away. Not when she was this close to unraveling the mystery, to finding the answers.

"I'm not afraid of the truth, Kai," she said, her voice trembling but determined. "I need to know. I need to understand what's happening to this place… to us."

A flicker of something crossed his face—resignation, perhaps, or maybe just the raw weight of the inevitable. With a heavy sigh, he reached out and cupped her face in his hands, his touch gentle, almost reverent. Lila's breath caught in her throat at the contact, the warmth of his skin against hers sending a jolt of electricity straight to her core.

"You should be afraid," he whispered, his voice strained. "Because once you know, there's no going back."

And then, before she could respond, the ship jerked again, throwing them both to the ground as the storm outside erupted with fury. The sound of wood groaning and the creaking of the hull were swallowed by the violent winds that tore at the ship, the violent shaking of the vessel rattling through their bones. Kai was on his feet in an instant, his hand gripping Lila's wrist with surprising force as he pulled her toward the stairs leading below deck.

"Stay with me," he said, his voice low, almost desperate. "We need to secure the ship. There's no telling how long this will last."

Lila's pulse raced as she followed him, feeling the tension in his grip, the urgency in his every movement. His eyes flicked to hers only briefly, but in that brief glance, she saw the fear that had been so carefully hidden behind his tough exterior. She saw something more than the man who had been pushing her away, something far more vulnerable. And for the first time, she realized that she wasn't just drawn to him because of the mystery of the sea—she was drawn to him because he, too, was a mystery she couldn't unravel. Yet.

They descended into the dark belly of the ship, the dim light flickering as the vessel swayed violently in the storm. Lila's heart raced, but her mind was focused, determined to get answers. The secrets Kai was hiding were buried too deep beneath the surface, but she wouldn't let them stay hidden much longer.

"I won't stop," she said softly, more to herself than to him.

Kai's grip on her hand tightened, his voice low, barely above a whisper. "I know."

And then the ship groaned again, louder this time, as though the sea was preparing to swallow them whole. Lila's stomach twisted in fear, but there was something else, something stronger than fear.

It was the pull of the ocean, the pull of the secrets beneath the waves. And no matter how much she fought it, she knew, deep down, that she was already too far gone.

Whispers Beneath the Waves

The wind howled above deck, a wailing beast of nature, as though it too were caught in the grip of something ancient and unforgiving. Below deck, the air was thick with the scent of salt and damp wood, the flickering lanterns casting restless shadows along the walls. Lila gripped the wooden railing, trying to steady herself against the sway of the ship, but it wasn't the rocking of the vessel that had her heart pounding. It was Kai.

She had lost him again.

Not physically—no, he was still here somewhere, moving through the darkened passages of the ship with the kind of silent intensity that sent shivers down her spine. But emotionally? He was a hundred miles away, locked behind a wall of secrets she had no hope of breaking down. Not yet, at least.

Lila bit her lip, frustration twisting in her gut. She had tried. Oh, how she had tried to reach him. Every word, every touch was a plea for him to open up, to let her in. But each time, she hit a wall—his guarded silence, the flashes of fear that flickered in his eyes before he quickly masked them with that distant look that had become his signature.

But tonight? Tonight, the storm outside seemed to reflect the storm within her. There was something different in the air, something thick and electric, as though the world was holding its breath in anticipation of the inevitable. The sea outside was no longer just churning—it was thrashing, its waves swelling and crashing in a fury that felt unnatural, too violent for any ordinary storm. Something was changing, something far more dangerous than the weather.

She needed to find him. She needed to understand why the sea was so restless, why it was calling to them both in ways that defied reason. And if it meant confronting Kai again, breaking through the walls he had built, then so be it.

Lila's boots clicked softly against the wood as she moved through the narrow hallways, each step echoing in the silence that seemed to have settled over the ship like a shroud. The smell of damp earth and seaweed filled her nostrils as she moved deeper into the belly of the ship, toward the small cabin where she had last seen him.

When she reached the door, she hesitated for a moment, her hand hovering over the handle. The storm outside was a beast, relentless and hungry, but it was nothing compared to the storm inside this ship, the storm between them. She pressed her hand to the door, steeling herself. There was no turning back now.

The door creaked open, revealing a dimly lit space. Kai stood by the small window, his back to her, his eyes fixed on the distant sea. His posture was rigid, his shoulders taut with the weight of whatever it was he was holding inside.

"Kai?" Lila's voice was quiet, soft, but it cut through the tension in the room like a knife.

He stiffened at the sound of her voice, but he didn't turn around. "Lila," he said, his tone cool and controlled, though she could hear the undercurrent of something—fear? Regret? It was hard to tell.

"I need to know what's happening," she said, her voice gaining strength. She stepped closer, her heartbeat quickening with every movement she made. "You've been shutting me out for days, Kai. I can't keep doing this. I'm not going to walk away from this without understanding what it is that you're hiding."

He turned slowly, his dark eyes meeting hers with an intensity that made her breath catch in her throat. "You don't want to know," he said, his voice low and thick, like the rumble of thunder on the horizon. "You think you're ready for this, Lila, but you're not. You're already in too deep."

"I don't care," she said, her voice trembling but firm. "I can't stand not knowing anymore. Please."

Kai's jaw tightened as he took a step toward her, his eyes never leaving hers. For a moment, it felt as though the world outside had faded away, as though nothing mattered except for the two of them standing in the dimly lit cabin, caught in the electric tension that pulsed between them. His breath was ragged, shallow, and Lila could see the conflict in his gaze—he wanted to pull her closer, to protect her from the truth, but something in her eyes stopped him. It wasn't pity she saw there. It was understanding. And maybe… maybe a little bit of something else.

"Lila," he whispered, his voice barely audible over the howling wind, "this town… this sea, it's all connected. We're not just dealing with a storm or some freak occurrence. We're dealing with something far older. Something that was buried long ago, but it's waking up now. And we—" He stopped, taking a deep breath, as if bracing himself. "We've awakened it."

The weight of his words settled over her like a heavy shroud, and Lila's pulse quickened, her stomach tightening in fear. She could feel the tension building, rising in her chest like a wave that refused to break. She reached out, her hand trembling as it touched his arm, the warmth of his skin radiating through the thin fabric of his shirt.

"We?" she asked softly, her voice barely above a whisper.

Kai's eyes flickered down to her hand before he turned his face away, his features hardening once again. "This wasn't just fate, Lila. It wasn't an accident that brought you here. You're tied to this—more than you realize. More than I ever wanted to admit."

Lila took a step back, her heart hammering in her chest as the words echoed in her mind. Tied to this? But how? Why?

"What do you mean?" Her voice cracked, but she swallowed hard, trying to push the fear down. She couldn't afford to be afraid. Not now. Not when the answers were so close.

Kai's expression softened for the briefest moment, a flicker of something raw and vulnerable crossing his face. But it was gone before she could fully grasp it. "The sea," he began slowly, his voice a low murmur, "it's not just a body of water. It's a force. It's been watching, waiting, and it knows… it knows about you, Lila. It knows about your family, your bloodline. This curse… this thing that's been haunting the town? It's been following you for generations."

Lila's breath hitched in her throat as the pieces began to fall into place. Her family. Her bloodline. It was always there, buried in the back of her mind, lurking in the corners of the stories she had heard growing up—of the curse, of the strange tides, of the inexplicable events that seemed to plague her lineage. But she had never truly believed it. She couldn't.

But now, standing here with Kai, feeling the weight of his words and the dark energy pressing against her chest, she realized the truth. This wasn't some tale spun by superstitious locals. This was real.

"What does it want from me?" Lila whispered, her voice barely audible, the fear creeping into her words despite her best efforts to remain calm.

Kai reached for her then, his hand grasping hers with an intensity that made her heart race. "It wants you to choose, Lila. Choose whether you'll let it consume you—or whether you'll try to stop it. But in the end, you'll lose either way."

His words were like ice, freezing her to the spot as the implications settled over her like a blanket of dread. She felt the pull of the sea again, that strange, magnetic force that had been gnawing at her ever since she arrived. She wasn't just a witness to this mystery. She was a part of it. And the sea was calling to her, beckoning her toward the deep, toward whatever it was that lay hidden beneath its waves.

Kai's hand tightened around hers, as if sensing her rising panic. "We have to stop this," he said urgently, his voice ragged with emotion. "Before it's too late."

Lila nodded, though she had no idea how they could stop it. She only knew that they had no time left. Whatever was coming—whatever had been awakened—was closer than either of them realized.

The ship groaned again, louder this time, as the wind picked up outside. The storm was reaching its peak, and with it, the unspoken tension between them cracked open. The sea was restless. The storm was closing in. And the secrets Kai had been holding for so long were finally beginning to surface.

And Lila knew, with chilling clarity, that there was no going back.

Crashing Surfaces

The ship creaked and groaned beneath Lila's feet as though it, too, was alive, caught in the thrashing waves of the storm that raged around them. The rain came down in sheets, a heavy, unrelenting deluge that blurred the line between sea and sky, casting the world in a haze of gray and white. Lila could barely hear her own thoughts over the roar of the wind, the howl of the ocean as it whipped against the hull, shaking the vessel with a violent intensity that made her heart race. But it wasn't the storm that unsettled her—it was Kai.

He had barely spoken since their conversation in the cabin. Since the moment he had told her that the sea was calling her. That her family, her bloodline, was tied to the curse that had haunted this place for generations. His words had echoed in her mind ever since, haunting her with their weight, their implications. She could feel the storm in the air, but she could also feel the storm between them. It was growing—dark, heavy, and charged with something she couldn't fully understand.

Lila stood at the railing, gripping it with both hands as the ship rocked violently beneath her. The sky had darkened even further, the clouds swirling above them like a vortex, and the water churned in eerie patterns beneath the surface. The air was thick with salt, the sting of it sharp against her skin, and every breath she took felt like a struggle against the suffocating pressure of the storm.

She could hear Kai behind her, his presence like a shadow in the midst of the storm, his silence a constant reminder that she was still waiting for him to tell her everything. To tell her what he was hiding, what he feared. But no matter how hard she tried to bridge the distance between them, he remained locked in his own world, a man running from something far deeper than the storm.

"Kai?" Her voice barely carried above the wind, but she knew he could hear her. She turned, her eyes searching for him through the rain-soaked air. There was no mistaking his silhouette, the way he stood with his back to her, staring out at the sea with a gaze that seemed to see something beyond the waves, something far darker than the raging storm.

He didn't answer at first, and for a moment, Lila felt a pang of frustration, of helplessness. But then, finally, he spoke, his voice low and strained, barely audible over the wind.

"You should go below deck," he said, without turning to face her. "It's too dangerous out here."

"I'm not going anywhere," she replied, her voice sharp, but there was something else beneath the words. Something soft, vulnerable. She wasn't afraid of the storm anymore. She wasn't afraid of what it was trying to drag out of her. "Not until you tell me what's really going on. What we are really dealing with here."

Kai's shoulders stiffened, and he turned slowly, his eyes narrowing as he looked at her. The intensity in his gaze almost knocked the breath out of her. "Lila…" he began, but his words faltered, his throat constricting as though the very air was choking him.

"What aren't you telling me, Kai?" she pressed, taking a step toward him, her heart hammering in her chest. "Why are you so afraid? You said the sea knows about me. About my family. What does that even mean?"

There was a flicker of something—fear? Regret?—in his eyes before he masked it with the same stoic expression that had become his trademark. But for the briefest of moments, Lila saw the truth in his eyes. She saw the pain, the burden, the darkness he was carrying, and for the first time, she didn't want to run from it. She wanted to carry it with him. She wanted to help him, even if it meant plunging deeper into the mystery that surrounded them both.

But then, just as quickly, the mask fell back into place.

"You don't want to know, Lila," Kai said, his voice low and rough. "It's not something you can understand."

The words stung, but Lila didn't let them deter her. She took another step toward him, closing the distance between them until they were standing so close that she could feel the heat radiating off him, could feel the tension in his body as though he were holding himself back from something. From her.

"I understand more than you think," she said, her voice soft but determined. "I know this place is cursed. I know there's something in the water, something that's been waiting for centuries. But you—" She swallowed hard, her throat tight. "You're the key, aren't you? Whatever's happening… it's because of you. And because of me."

Kai's eyes flickered to hers for a moment, something unreadable flashing across his features. Then, with a sudden, almost violent motion, he reached out and grabbed her arm, pulling her closer, his grip firm and desperate.

"You don't know what you're saying," he muttered, his breath warm against her skin. "You don't understand how dangerous this is. How dangerous you are."

Lila's heart skipped a beat, the words sinking into her chest like a stone. She opened her mouth to respond, to demand an explanation, but before she could speak, a sudden, violent shudder ran through the ship. The sound of the hull groaning under the pressure of the waves was deafening, and for a split second, everything seemed to tilt at a sharp angle. Lila gasped, her heart lurching in her chest as the ship tilted dangerously.

"Hold on!" Kai shouted, his voice cutting through the chaos, but it was too late.

The next moment, the ship lurched again, the deck beneath her feet shifting violently, sending her sprawling toward the edge. Her heart hammered in her chest as the ship tilted even further, the world spinning around her in a dizzying whirl of water and storm. She tried to reach out, to grab hold of something, but her body was thrown forward, and her hand gripped nothing but empty air.

"Lila!" Kai's voice broke through the fog of panic, and suddenly, his hand was there, pulling her back, steadying her with a force that sent a shock through her body. His grip was tight, almost painful, but she didn't care. She clung to him, feeling the strength of his hold, the urgency in his movements as he pulled her back toward the center of the deck.

Her breath came in ragged gasps, and she could feel the cold, damp air biting at her skin as she pressed herself against him. The storm was no longer just a force of nature—it was alive, a creature that had come to claim them, to drag them under. The ship was fighting to stay afloat, but the storm was relentless, its fury pushing against them with an almost malevolent intent.

Lila's heart was still racing, but she could feel Kai's steady pulse beneath her hand, the warmth of his body against hers as he held her tight, his voice low and urgent in her ear.

"We need to get below," he said, his breath ragged. "It's not safe here. We're not alone anymore."

At his words, a chill ran down her spine, colder than the wind that whipped around them. Not alone. The words seemed to echo in her mind as she looked out at the raging sea, the waters swirling with a dark energy, pulling at the ship as though it were nothing more than a toy in the hands of a monstrous force.

"Kai, what do you mean?" she asked, her voice trembling with both fear and confusion. "What's happening? What's out there?"

His gaze flickered toward the horizon, where the water seemed to boil and seethe, the waves rising impossibly high, as though they were reaching for the heavens themselves. His jaw tightened, and Lila could see the fear in his eyes, despite the control he was fighting to maintain.

"It's the sea," he said, his voice barely above a whisper, his words almost lost in the wind. "It's not just the storm anymore. Something… something else is coming. And it's coming for you."

The words hung in the air between them, heavy with a truth neither of them was ready to face. And just as quickly, the ship shuddered once more, throwing them both to the ground as the sky seemed to open up above them.

And then the world went black.

Falling into the Current

The moment the world righted itself, Lila's senses exploded into overdrive—her heart still hammering in her chest, the sound of the wind roaring like a thousand whispers of warning, the crash of waves against the hull like the pounding of an angry drum. She sat up quickly, disoriented, the edges of the world still swimming as the ship groaned and shuddered beneath her. The cold, damp air pressed against her skin, and she shivered, not from the temperature but from the overwhelming pressure that seemed to settle over the ship.

She blinked, trying to focus, but everything seemed to be moving too quickly, the storm spinning around her, the water threatening to swallow the ship whole. She could barely hear her own thoughts over the cacophony of sound, but there was one thing that pierced through it all—Kai.

His hand had been on her wrist the moment the ship had lurched, and though she hadn't realized it until now, he had dragged her with him as the boat tilted, keeping her steady, keeping her grounded in a chaos that was threatening to swallow them whole.

"Kai?" Her voice cracked against the wind, strained and thin. Her hand reached out blindly, searching for him, and then, as though the storm had decided to take pity on her, she saw him— standing at the edge of the ship, one hand gripping the railing, his gaze fixed on something out in the storm, his silhouette dark against the raging sky.

"Kai!" she called again, this time louder, pushing herself to her feet with the force of her words. The ship gave another violent lurch, and she had to steady herself with the railing. Her hand clutched it so tightly that her knuckles turned white.

He didn't turn, but she could see his posture stiffen. The tension between them—always there, like an invisible thread pulling them together and tearing them apart—was palpable. She could almost feel it humming in the air, an undercurrent to the storm's fury.

Without another word, she moved toward him, her boots heavy against the deck, her every step an effort to stay grounded as the wind lashed at her face, the spray of saltwater stinging her skin. The ship was fighting against the storm, but so were they, both caught in a current they couldn't escape.

"Why won't you tell me what's happening?" she demanded, her

voice sharper than she intended as she reached him, her fingers brushing against his arm. She was close enough now to feel the heat of his body, the raw tension in the way he held himself—his back taut, his jaw clenched, his eyes still trained on the churning sea.

He didn't answer right away, and for a brief moment, it felt as though the storm itself was holding its breath, waiting for him to speak. His body seemed to vibrate with something, an energy that Lila couldn't identify, but she felt it in her own chest, an answering beat to the storm's fury.

"We can't outrun this," Kai finally said, his voice rough, as though he hadn't spoken in days. "This—whatever it is—it's not just coming for the ship. It's coming for us."

Lila's stomach dropped, the words seeping into her skin like cold water. Her hand tightened on his arm, and for the briefest moment, he flinched, as if her touch had burned him, but then he let her hold him, his muscles relaxing just enough to let her in. But she could feel the walls still, thick and unyielding.

"What is it? What's coming?" she asked, the fear in her voice now as raw and jagged as the storm itself. The uncertainty—the terror—swept over her, and she couldn't push it away. Not anymore.

Kai turned to face her then, his dark eyes meeting hers with such intensity that it nearly took her breath away. The storm howled around them, but there was a moment of silence, a heartbeat where nothing existed except the two of them, caught between the storm above and the ocean below.

"I don't know what it is," he said, his voice a whisper against the roar of the sea. "But it knows about us. About you."

Lila's heart beat faster at the weight of his words, and she stepped closer, her eyes narrowing as she tried to catch the elusive glint of truth in his words. But it wasn't the storm that was making her dizzy—it was the way he was looking at her, as though she was both the answer and the key, the one thing that could either save them or destroy them.

"I've been trying to protect you," Kai continued, his voice rough with emotion, but there was something else there, something buried beneath the surface. "Trying to keep you away from it. But you're already too far in. The sea knows your name, Lila. It knows your blood."

She felt a cold shiver run down her spine at his words. The sea knows your blood—it wasn't just a warning anymore. It was a truth, one that settled over her like a stone. She had always known there was something darker in the air, something she couldn't explain. But now, it felt as though the storm was the sea's voice, speaking to her, calling to her with a ferocity she couldn't understand.

"What do you mean, it knows my blood?" Lila whispered, her fingers curling into his jacket, desperate to hold onto the only solid thing in this storm, in this world that was turning sideways with each passing moment.

His gaze softened just for a moment, and she saw something flicker behind his eyes—regret, maybe, or was it fear? His lips parted, but before he could speak, the ship lurched again, sending them both off balance. They crashed into the railing, Lila's chest slamming into it with a sharp gasp, and for a moment, she thought the ship might break apart under the strain of the storm.

She gasped for breath, but before she could regain her bearings, Kai's hand was there, steadying her, pulling her back against him, his body hard against hers as they both struggled to stay upright. Her pulse thundered in her ears, the smell of salt and rain surrounding them, but it was the heat of his body that drove all other thoughts from her mind.

"I've been fighting this," he said suddenly, his voice hoarse, his breath ragged against her ear. His hands were on her arms now, gripping her with a force that felt like a promise, an unspoken plea. "Fighting you. Because I can't let you fall into this. Into me."

Lila's breath caught, the words settling over her like a heavy blanket, stifling and suffocating. She didn't know what he meant, not fully, but she knew the storm wasn't just outside anymore. It was inside him, inside them both, tearing at them, pulling them toward something they didn't understand.

She turned in his arms then, forcing him to meet her gaze, her fingers digging into his jacket, her heart beating faster with each second they stood there, wrapped in the tension that hung between them like a fog.

"You don't get to push me away anymore," she said, her voice shaking, but determined. "Whatever this is, we're in it together, Kai. We have to face it. Together."

For a moment, Kai's eyes softened, just the slightest flicker of something like relief crossing his features, before it was buried again beneath a layer of hard resolve. He took a deep breath, his chest rising and falling beneath her hand, and then, slowly, he nodded.

"You're right," he whispered, his voice barely audible over the howling wind. "But this—this isn't over. And when it ends, I can't promise you'll want to be here anymore."

Lila's heart ached at his words, but there was something else there, something stronger than the fear that twisted in her gut. The pull between them had always been undeniable, but now it was something more. It was fate, intertwined with the sea and the storm. And no matter how dangerous it was, she wouldn't walk away. Not now.

"Then we'll see it through," she said, her voice steady, her heart a fierce rhythm in her chest. "We'll see it through to the end."

Kai's eyes held hers for a long moment, and for the first time, Lila saw something shift within him—something soft, something fragile—and in that moment, she knew. She knew the sea wasn't the only thing calling to them.

They were both already too far gone.

And there was no going back.

45

Eight

The Tide Turns

The night was suffocating, heavy with tension, as though the world itself were bracing for something immense. The storm had raged for days now, the ship creaking under the pressure, but it wasn't just the storm that made Lila's pulse race—it was the feeling that something was coming, something inevitable.

She stood at the helm, her fingers gripping the cold, slick wheel, her eyes straining against the blackened sea. The wind howled around her, making it feel as if the ocean were alive, reaching for her, begging her to come closer, to surrender to it. But Lila couldn't. Not yet.

Behind her, she could hear Kai's footsteps, the soft thud of his boots against the wood. He had been quieter than usual, but there was an underlying urgency to his movements, a sharpness in the way he moved that set Lila's nerves on edge. She didn't need to turn to know that he was standing there, watching her, his gaze heavy on her back. She could feel the weight of his presence even before she caught the fleeting warmth of his breath against her neck.

"You're not going to find anything out here, you know," he said, his voice low and strained, as though he were trying to pull her away from something too dangerous to face.

Lila didn't answer right away. Instead, she took another deep breath, inhaling the salt of the sea, the rawness of the storm that whipped around her. She had to know. She had to understand what was happening. What they were becoming.

"I'm not looking for anything," she finally said, her voice a mixture of defiance and something softer, something that caught in her throat. "I'm looking for the truth."

There was a long pause, the silence between them stretching out like a thread ready to snap. Then, with a sharp exhale, Kai moved closer, his boots echoing on the wooden deck as he stepped up beside her, his broad form standing just a breath away. The air between them seemed to hum, charged with the electricity of the storm and the weight of unspoken words.

"The truth is something you don't want to know, Lila," he said, his voice gravelly, the usual hardness gone, replaced with something that almost sounded like pleading. "You think you can handle it, but you can't. Not now. Not when it's this close."

Lila swallowed, her throat tight. She knew that he was right—that there was no going back from the truth—but she couldn't stop now. Not when the pull of the ocean was growing stronger with every passing moment, not when the strange connection between her and Kai was beginning to make her question everything she had ever known about herself.

"I've already seen more than I should," she whispered, her gaze never leaving the roiling waves. "But I need to know what this is. What you are."

Kai stiffened beside her, his breath catching in his throat at her words. She could feel the shift in him, the moment when the walls he had so carefully built around himself began to crumble. He didn't answer immediately, but she saw the way his jaw clenched, the way his hand twitched at his side as though he were struggling with something too large to contain.

"You're asking me to tell you things I can't," he said after a beat, his voice low, his words like gravel. "I've tried to protect you. I've tried to keep you safe from the truth because it'll destroy you, Lila. And I can't watch you break."

Lila's heart pounded in her chest, the words hitting her like a wave. She turned to face him then, her hands gripping the wheel so tightly her fingers ached. His gaze met hers, dark and full of the same intensity that had always pulled her to him, the same rawness that she couldn't seem to escape.

"You don't get to protect me anymore," she said, her voice fierce, her eyes burning with a determination she hadn't known she had. "I'm already in this, Kai. I'm already in you. And I can't walk away until I know everything."

The silence that followed was thick, suffocating. Lila could feel the storm inside him, a quiet rage, an endless conflict that seemed to mirror the fury of the ocean around them. She could hear the breath catch in his chest, the rapid beat of his heart that seemed to match her own. And then, finally, he moved.

His hand reached for hers, and for a moment, she thought he was going to pull away. But instead, he wrapped his fingers around hers, his touch warm and firm, grounding her in the chaos of the moment. His eyes were dark, unreadable, but there was something in them now—something softer, more vulnerable—that made her stomach tighten.

"You don't know what you're asking for," Kai said, his voice barely above a whisper. "But I can't let you go without the truth. I can't keep lying to you."

The words hung in the air between them, heavy and irrevocable, and Lila felt the weight of them settle deep within her chest, sinking into her bones. She didn't know how far she was willing to go, how much she was willing to sacrifice for this truth, but she knew she couldn't turn back. She couldn't walk away now, not when everything—everything—was pulling her toward it.

"You're not lying to me," she said, her voice fierce, her heart pounding in her chest. "You're trying to protect me from the truth, but the truth is mine to know. And I'll take whatever it costs."

For a moment, they stood there, locked in place, the storm raging around them, their fingers intertwined, the air between them thick with both the heat of their bodies and the tension that crackled in the space between them. The sound of the ocean was deafening now, the waves crashing against the hull with a ferocity that shook the ship to its core, as though the sea itself were alive, alive and watching them.

And then, with a breath that seemed to come from the depths of his soul, Kai spoke again, his voice low and raw.

"It's not just the sea," he said, his words laced with a bitterness that made her stomach twist. "It's the curse. My family—our families—they made a bargain with the sea centuries ago. A bargain that bound us to it. To the ocean's will. And you— Lila—you're part of it. You're a part of me now. And when the tide turns, it'll take you both. The sea… it won't stop until it's taken everything."

Lila felt her breath catch in her throat, the weight of his words crashing over her like a wave. She staggered backward, her hands gripping the railing to keep her steady as the truth settled into her chest like a stone.

"You…" Her voice trembled as she spoke, her pulse quickening. "You've been protecting me from this? From you?"

Kai's gaze hardened, his grip on her hand tightening almost painfully. "I didn't want you to know. Not like this. Not until I could protect you. But I see now that I can't keep you away from it. From what we are. From what we've become."

The world seemed to hold its breath as the storm raged around them, the ship rocking violently beneath their feet, as if the ocean itself were listening, waiting for something.

"You're right," Kai said quietly, his voice strained. "You're in this now. And so am I. We can't outrun it anymore. Not the sea. Not the curse. Not us."

Lila's heart thundered in her chest as the truth settled in her bones. She was in this. She was already too far gone, pulled into something far larger than herself, something she couldn't escape. The sea was calling to her, and it was coming for them both.

And there was no turning back now.

Nine

Tides of Betrayal

The night seemed endless. The storm had raged without pause for what felt like weeks, the ship groaning beneath the weight of the ocean's fury. Lila stood at the edge of the deck, her coat soaked through, her fingers numb against the cold metal of the railing. The wind howled around her, ripping at her hair, but she didn't move. The sea stretched before her, a vast, unyielding blackness, and she could feel it pulling her—calling her with a hunger that she couldn't ignore.

She had come so far, learned so much, but it was never enough. The storm, the secrets buried beneath the waves, and the curse— every revelation felt like a piece of the puzzle, yet it was still incomplete. There were things Kai had yet to tell her, things that twisted in her gut, and the more she thought about them, the more she realized that she couldn't trust anyone in this town, not even him.

Her heart ached as she thought of Kai. She could feel the weight of his absence now, his silence in the cabin below, the way he had retreated from her ever since their last conversation. The pull between them was undeniable, the fire that burned in her veins whenever they were close. But there was something else there too—a distance, a wall between them that had only grown thicker. Every time she tried to reach for him, to understand what he was hiding, he shut her out, and the more she tried to break through, the more she felt like she was drowning in a sea of lies.

She couldn't keep running from it. She had to know the truth, whatever it cost.

Suddenly, the sound of footsteps reached her ears, heavy and purposeful, the rhythmic crunch of boots against the soaked wood. Lila didn't need to turn to know who it was. Her heart skipped in her chest, a jolt of both fear and longing. Kai.

He appeared beside her, his silhouette dark against the storm, and for a long moment, neither of them spoke. The wind whipped around them, but the tension between them was thicker than the storm itself, an invisible thread binding them together despite the miles of space that had opened between them.

"You're not going to find any answers out here," Kai's voice broke through the silence, hoarse, and laced with something she couldn't quite place. His eyes flicked to the waves, then back to her, his expression unreadable.

"I'm not looking for answers," she replied, her voice firm but soft, the cold air biting at her words. "I'm looking for the truth."

Kai's jaw tightened, and for a moment, the storm seemed to pause around them, holding its breath. The world around them felt like it was holding its breath too, waiting for the moment that would change everything.

"What truth?" he asked, his tone darker now, the weight of his question hanging heavy between them. He stepped closer, just a fraction, but it was enough to make Lila's heart race faster. His presence, always so magnetic, was more intense than ever, his energy crackling in the air like static.

Lila's hands gripped the railing tighter, as if the ship itself might slip beneath her feet if she let go. "The truth about you," she said, her voice barely a whisper, yet the words felt like thunder in her chest. "About the curse. About the ocean. About what you've been hiding from me."

Kai's face remained stoic, but his eyes—dark and distant— flickered with something else. Something Lila couldn't read, but something that made her stomach twist. She took a step toward him, her boots heavy against the wet wood, her gaze never leaving his.

"You don't know what you're asking," Kai said, his voice low, but she could hear the desperation in it, the edge of something breaking. "The truth isn't something you can just take. It's dangerous, Lila. You think you're ready, but you're not. No one ever is."

"I'm not afraid," she whispered back, but her voice betrayed her—shaking just slightly, the vulnerability creeping through. "I'm in this already. I've been in this since I stepped onto this ship. You can't keep pushing me away."

Kai looked at her for a long, painful moment, his gaze flicking between her eyes and the dark horizon beyond them, as if he were battling some invisible force. And then, finally, he spoke, his voice raw with emotion.

"The sea knows you," he said, his words like a curse, a confession, and a warning all at once. "It's not just the storm. It's what's beneath the surface. It's what's coming for you."

Lila's breath caught in her throat, her body stiffening at his words. She had always felt it—the pull, the whispers beneath the waves—but hearing him say it, hearing him confirm her fears, sent a chill down her spine.

"What do you mean?" she asked, her voice trembling now, the words barely making it past her lips. She reached for him, her hand shaking as she placed it on his arm. "Kai, please… tell me. I need to know."

Kai didn't move, his eyes flicking to her hand, then to her face, his expression torn. He swallowed hard, the tension in his jaw betraying his inner conflict. And then, with a sigh that felt like the weight of the world, he pulled her closer, his hands gripping her arms, holding her steady as he looked into her eyes—really looked into her eyes—for the first time in days.

"You're tied to this," he said, his voice almost a whisper, as though the words themselves were dangerous. "Tied to me. And once the sea has marked you, it never lets you go."

Lila felt her heart skip a beat, the world around them fading as his words sank in. The storm roared around them, but it seemed far away, as if everything had receded except for the two of them and the weight of the truth hanging between them.

"You're part of it, Lila," he continued, his voice strained. "The curse. The ocean. Everything. Your blood, your family… it's all connected. It's always been connected. And now—now you're caught in it. Caught in us."

The air between them felt thick, suffocating, but Lila couldn't pull away. She couldn't move, not with the way his hands held her, not with the way his eyes searched hers, as though looking for something—anything—to make sense of this, to make sense of them.

"I don't understand," she said softly, her voice barely above a whisper. "What does that mean? What does it mean for me?"

Kai's grip on her tightened, pulling her even closer until she could feel the heat of his body pressing against hers, the urgency in his touch. "It means that the sea won't stop until it has you. Until it pulls you under. And there's nothing I can do to stop it, Lila. Nothing."

Lila's breath hitched in her throat, the weight of his words sinking in deeper with every second. She had always known, in some part of her, that the sea was calling her—but hearing him say it out loud, hearing him say that the ocean would stop at nothing to claim her, made her heart stutter in her chest.

"But what about you?" she asked, her voice thick with emotion. "What about us?"

Kai's eyes softened for the briefest moment, but then they hardened again, his jaw clenching as he pulled back just slightly, as though the weight of the truth was too much to bear.

"I'm not enough to save you, Lila," he said quietly, the words like a blow to her chest. "I've tried to protect you, but I can't fight this. I can't fight what's coming."

Lila took a step back, her heart shattering as the full weight of his words sank in. The space between them grew, and for the first time in what felt like forever, she felt an icy distance growing between them, a gulf that neither of them could cross.

"You said we were in this together," she said, her voice shaking, but she held her ground. "You said we couldn't outrun this. So why are you pushing me away?"

Kai's eyes flashed with something raw—anger, regret, or maybe a mixture of both—but he didn't answer her. Instead, he turned, stepping away, his back to her as he faced the storm, his shoulders hunched as though the weight of the world had settled on them.

"You don't understand," he muttered, more to himself than to her. "You can't understand."

Lila stood there, the space between them more painful than any distance she had ever known. The ocean roared behind them, but it wasn't the storm that terrified her—it was the man she had come to love, the man who had just told her that there was no way out.

And for the first time, Lila realized that the greatest danger wasn't the sea, wasn't the curse—it was the man who held her heart and was now pushing her away.

And she didn't know if she could save him. Or herself.

Ten

Beneath the Moonlit Waves

The moon hung low in the sky, a pale, silvery eye watching over the restless sea. The night was eerily still, the storm's fury having calmed, but the air still hummed with a tension that made Lila's skin crawl. The ship rocked gently on the water, its creaking sounds now muted compared to the thundering chaos of the days before. But the quiet was just as oppressive, suffocating in its own way, as if the world itself was waiting for something. For her.

She stood at the edge of the deck, her eyes trained on the horizon, where the water seemed to shimmer beneath the moon's cold light. The air was thick with salt, the scent of the ocean seeping into her skin, her lungs, but it was more than the scent of the sea. It was the weight of the secrets she had uncovered, the looming truth she still didn't fully understand, and the strange pull she felt inside her, as if the ocean were reaching for her, calling her to the depths.

Behind her, she could hear the soft footfalls of someone approaching. Her heart skipped a beat, and she didn't have to turn to know it was Kai. She could feel him, feel the way the space between them seemed to crackle with something—something both dangerous and magnetic. She didn't need to ask if he had been watching her. She could sense his presence, always lurking, always just behind her, waiting for the right moment to strike. But tonight, she was done waiting. Tonight, the truth would finally surface.

She didn't turn to face him immediately. Instead, she leaned over the railing, her fingers gripping it tightly, as if holding on to something real, something solid in the storm of emotions that churned inside her. The night was alive with the sounds of the sea, the distant cry of gulls, the lap of water against the hull, but there was something else—something she couldn't name, but felt deep within her bones. The sea, the curse, Kai—everything was connected, everything was converging in this moment, and she didn't know if she was ready for it.

Finally, Kai's voice broke the silence, low and rough, filled with a depth that made her blood run cold.

"You shouldn't be out here alone." His words were an almost imperceptible tremor in the heavy air, his tone edged with something she couldn't read. Concern? Fear? Maybe both.

Lila slowly turned to face him, her heart racing as she met his gaze. His face was partially illuminated by the pale moonlight, casting shadows across his sharp features, making him look even more otherworldly, almost untouchable. But beneath the intensity in his eyes, Lila saw something else—something raw, something that tore at her heart. The vulnerability he had tried so desperately to hide.

"I don't need protecting," she said, her voice steady, though it faltered just slightly, betraying the emotions that swirled beneath the surface. "Not from you. Not anymore."

For a long moment, Kai didn't speak. He just stood there, watching her, his expression unreadable. The distance between them was palpable, but it wasn't just physical. It was a gulf that had grown between them over the course of the last few days, a divide created by the secrets they had yet to share, the things they couldn't say. And as much as Lila wanted to break through it, she didn't know if she could. Not anymore.

"You don't know what you're dealing with," Kai finally said, his voice low, almost to himself. "I tried to protect you from this, from the truth. I never wanted you to be a part of it. But now, it's too late."

Lila felt the chill creep up her spine at his words, her fingers tightening on the railing, but she forced herself to stay calm. She had come this far. She couldn't turn back now.

"You keep saying that," she said, her voice barely above a whisper, but it was stronger than she felt. "What truth, Kai? What is it that you're so afraid of? What are we running from?"

Kai's eyes flickered to the horizon, his gaze distant, as if the sea held the answers he was too afraid to speak. "It's not something you can run from," he said quietly, his voice filled with regret. "It's already too deep inside you. It always has been. And I—I'm the one who brought you here. I'm the one who couldn't stay away."

Lila's heart skipped in her chest at his words. The pain in his voice, the way it cracked as he spoke—everything about him in that moment felt like it was unraveling. The walls he had so carefully constructed were crumbling, piece by piece, leaving him exposed, vulnerable. And she hated that she was the one causing it, even though a part of her knew she had to be.

"What does that mean?" she asked, her voice trembling now. "What do you mean, 'you brought me here'? You—"

Before she could finish, the ship lurched violently, throwing them both off balance. Lila gasped, her feet slipping as the world tilted beneath her, and for a moment, everything went black, the night and the sea spinning together in a dizzying whirl of water and wind. Her breath caught in her throat as she flailed, but strong arms wrapped around her, pulling her back to safety, steadying her against the storm.

Kai's face was inches from hers, his hands on her arms, his grip firm, his body heat radiating into hers like an anchor in the chaos. His eyes, dark and intense, locked onto hers, and for a moment, everything else disappeared. The storm, the ocean, the secrets—they were gone, nothing left but the two of them, standing on the edge of the world, caught in the current of something neither of them could control.

"Don't ever do that again," Kai whispered, his breath ragged as he pulled her closer, his hands tightening around her, as if he feared she might slip away.

"I won't," she breathed, her voice barely audible, her chest tight with the intensity of the moment. The air around them crackled with something electric, something magnetic that neither of them could fight. "I'm not going anywhere, Kai. Not anymore."

His eyes searched hers, his face still so close to hers that she could feel the heat of his breath on her skin. "You should," he said quietly, his voice raw. "You should walk away before it's too late. Before you're too deep."

But Lila didn't move. She couldn't. She had already made her choice. She was already in this, caught between the sea, the curse, and the man who had somehow become both her salvation and her destruction. She could feel the pull of the ocean deep inside her, its dark promise reaching for her, tugging at her like an undertow.

"I'm not afraid of you, Kai," she whispered, her voice thick with emotion. "I'm not afraid of this anymore. I know what's happening, what I'm tied to. And I'm not running. Not from you."

Kai's grip on her tightened, his eyes flickering with something close to pain. "You don't know what you're asking for," he whispered, his voice hoarse. "The sea... it's not just going to take you. It's going to take everything."

Lila's heart pounded in her chest, the weight of his words sinking into her like a stone. She could feel the truth of them, like an unspoken promise, but she didn't pull away. Instead, she leaned in, her breath mingling with his as she closed the space between them.

"I'm ready," she said, her voice steady, even though her insides were twisting with fear. "I'm ready to face it. With you."

For a moment, they stood there, locked together in a silence that felt like a promise, the world around them swirling in chaos. The moonlight gleamed down on them, casting everything in its cold, silvery glow, and for the first time, Lila felt as if the sea had finally claimed her.

But just as quickly as the calm had settled over them, it shattered. A low, eerie growl rumbled from the depths of the ocean, a sound so deep, so ancient, that it sent a shiver of terror through her. The sea seemed to tremble, as though something was stirring beneath the surface, something vast, something powerful.

And then, from the depths, something rose.

Lila's breath caught in her throat as the water seemed to swirl, coiling like a serpent beneath them. She felt the pull, a force stronger than gravity, pulling her toward it, drawing her closer to the heart of the ocean.

Kai's hand gripped hers tighter, pulling her back, but Lila knew. She knew that whatever was coming, whatever had been waiting for her beneath the surface, had finally found her.

And she wasn't ready to run anymore.

The tide had turned.

And there was no going back.

Eleven

Rising Storm

The waves lashed against the hull, their violent slaps like
fists pounding against the ship's fragile shell. Lila's
breath hitched in her chest as she gripped the railing,
her fingers aching from the tightness of her hold. The night
was a nightmare of noise, a constant roar that threatened to
swallow the world whole. The storm had come back with a
vengeance—fury crashing down on them from all sides, as if
the sea itself were trying to tear them apart. The dark waters
churned, twisting in unnatural patterns that made Lila's pulse
race with both fear and fascination.

She could feel it. The pull. The call of the ocean, deeper now
than ever before. It wasn't just the sea. It was something ancient,
something vast, something far beyond her understanding. The
curse, the ocean's will, the secrets Kai had tried so hard to
protect her from—everything was coming to a head, and she

could no longer pretend that she could outrun it.

The sound of footsteps behind her broke her concentration, and she turned, already knowing who it was before she even saw him. Kai. His figure loomed tall and dark in the shadow of the storm, his coat whipping violently around his body as he moved toward her, his eyes never leaving the horizon. His presence was magnetic, always pulling her in, but now, there was something in his eyes—something that both terrified and enthralled her.

"You shouldn't be out here," Kai said, his voice rough and strained, cutting through the cacophony of wind and water. His words were half-lost in the storm, but she could feel the weight behind them, the urgency in his tone. "It's not safe."

Lila glanced back at him, feeling the tension between them crackle in the air, thick and palpable. She had heard those words before, but they no longer held the same power over her. She was in this now. She was already too deep, caught in the current of this storm, this curse, and whatever the ocean was hiding beneath its depths.

"I'm not afraid of the storm," she replied, her voice steady despite the fear tightening her chest. "I'm not afraid of you either, Kai."

His eyes flickered to hers, a sharp, pained look passing through them before he turned his gaze back to the raging sea. His jaw clenched, his body tense, as if he was fighting something inside of himself—something he couldn't let go of, something that was holding him back from telling her everything. She could see it in the way he moved, the way he was always so carefully guarding himself, as if the truth was something too dangerous to reveal. But it was already too late. The truth was already in the air between them, hanging like a stormcloud, ready to burst.

"I told you to stay away," he said, his voice almost a growl, the desperation leaking through despite his best efforts. "I told you not to get involved in this. It's too dangerous."

Lila took a step closer to him, her breath ragged, her chest tight with a mix of fear and desire. She wanted to understand— needed to understand what was happening, what he was hiding from her. She couldn't ignore the pull anymore. The ocean wasn't just calling to her. It was pulling them both in, and she could feel it tightening its grip with every passing second.

"You don't get to make that decision for me," she whispered, her voice soft but firm. "Not anymore."

Kai turned to her then, his face inches from hers, the storm seeming to fade into the background, as if nothing else existed but the two of them. His eyes searched hers with an intensity that made her breath catch in her throat. His hands reached for her, pulling her close, his touch fierce, as if he couldn't bear the thought of losing her. She felt the heat of him against her, the storm of his emotions crashing around them, just as violently as the storm outside.

"You think you're ready for this?" he asked, his voice low, almost a growl. His lips were close to hers now, and Lila could feel the warmth of his breath mingling with her own. "You think you're ready to face the truth?"

Lila's heart raced in her chest, her fingers gripping his coat, pulling him even closer. She could feel the beat of his heart beneath her hand, the thrum of his pulse like a drum, steady and insistent. "I don't care what the truth is," she said, her voice trembling with something she couldn't name. "I need to know. I need to know what's happening."

For a moment, there was nothing but the pounding of their hearts and the sound of the storm. The space between them was electric, charged with everything they had never said. Lila knew that they were standing on the edge of something—something they couldn't escape, no matter how hard they tried.

"Lila…" Kai's voice cracked, a sharp edge of fear creeping into it. "You're already too far gone. I can't protect you from this. Not from me."

Her heart dropped, the words like ice running through her veins. "What do you mean?" she whispered, her voice barely audible over the storm's roar.

Kai's grip on her tightened, his face a mask of conflict and torment. "The sea isn't just pulling us in," he said, his voice hoarse, raw with emotion. "It's pulling you. You're part of this. You always have been. And I—I'm the one who brought you here."

Lila's breath caught in her throat as the truth began to settle over her, heavy and suffocating. She had known, in some deep part of herself, that this was more than just a story, more than just a curse—it was about her, and it was about Kai. They were caught in this, tangled in a web that neither of them had chosen, but both of them were now trapped in.

"The curse," she whispered, her mind racing as everything began to click into place. "The curse isn't just something that's been passed down through the generations. It's tied to us, isn't it?"

Kai's eyes darkened, his jaw tight as he nodded slowly. "It's always been tied to us. To you."

Lila stepped back, her heart thudding in her chest as the weight of his words crushed her. She had been so caught up in the storm outside, in the fury of the sea, that she hadn't realized that the true storm was inside of them, between them. The ocean wasn't just calling to her—it was calling to them both. And it wasn't going to stop until it had them.

"What happens when it takes us?" Lila asked, her voice trembling, though she refused to back down.

Kai's eyes softened for a moment, and for the first time, she saw the raw vulnerability in him, the pain that he had been hiding so carefully. But it was gone before she could hold on to it, replaced by something colder, more distant. He shook his head, as if he couldn't bear to speak the words.

"It'll take everything," he said, his voice flat, void of emotion. "And when it's done, nothing will be left. Not you. Not me.

Nothing."

The words hit her like a physical blow, her chest tightening with the weight of what he was saying. She wanted to scream, to demand that they find a way out, but she didn't know if there was a way out anymore. The ocean had already claimed them. And she wasn't sure if she was ready to fight it.

"You're not going to stop me," Lila said, her voice stronger than she felt, her eyes never leaving his. "I'm already too deep, Kai. I'm already part of this. And I'm not running."

For a moment, Kai didn't say anything. He just looked at her, his eyes dark with something she couldn't decipher. Then, slowly, he took a step back, releasing her from his grasp. His hands fell to his sides, and for the first time, Lila saw the true weight of what they were both facing.

"You don't know what you're asking for," he said, his voice distant now, cold. "But you're right. You can't run from it. Neither of us can."

The sea howled around them, its roar growing louder, as if it were listening to their words, watching them. Lila's heart pounded in her chest, the reality of their situation sinking in. They were bound to this. To each other, to the curse, to the sea. And no matter how much they fought, it would claim them in the end.

But Lila wasn't ready to give up. Not yet. Not when there was still a chance to change the course of the storm.

"I'm ready for whatever comes next," she said, her voice steady, her eyes locked on Kai's. "We're in this together."

Kai's gaze flickered over her, a flicker of something—hope?—before it disappeared, buried under the weight of the storm. He nodded once, a silent agreement between them, and for a moment, Lila thought she saw a glimmer of something else in his eyes. Something softer, something that made her heart twist with longing.

But then the storm roared again, louder, the waves crashing against the ship, and everything else faded away.

The tide was rising.

And they were both caught in its current.

Twelve

Love's Final Tide

The storm raged with a fury that seemed to reach the very soul of the world, the sky flashing with violent streaks of lightning, the thunder a roar that reverberated through the bones of the ship. Lila stood at the edge of the deck, her hands gripping the wet railing, her coat soaked through and heavy against her skin. The wind howled around her, tugging at her hair, as if the storm itself were trying to pull her under, into the churning depths of the ocean below. The water had turned black, swallowing the ship whole, as if the sea were conspiring against them, determined to drag them into its dark, unforgiving embrace.

Lila's heart raced, but it wasn't just the storm that set her pulse thumping in her chest—it was the man standing just a few feet away, the man whose presence had been the only constant in this chaos, whose touch had both burned and healed her. Kai.

He was standing in the shadow of the wheelhouse, his dark eyes flickering toward her, though he didn't move. His posture was rigid, tense, as if he were waiting for something—waiting for the inevitable to crash down on them both. She could feel the weight of the tension between them, thick and suffocating, like a heavy fog. She knew what he was feeling—what he had been feeling since the night she had first set foot on this cursed ship. He was trying to protect her. Trying to keep her safe. But now, there was no running from it, no hiding from the truth.

She stepped toward him, her boots squelching in the rain-soaked wood, her gaze never leaving his face. The intensity of the storm around them was nothing compared to the storm that had been brewing between them, the one that had been building ever since they had met. The magnetic pull between them had only grown stronger with each passing hour, each desperate breath they took, but the closer she got to him, the more she could see the walls he had built around himself. He was afraid to let her in. He was afraid of what they were becoming.

"You're still trying to protect me," she said softly, her voice barely audible over the roar of the wind. "From everything. From this."

Kai's expression hardened, but there was a flicker of something in his eyes—something deep and painful that made her stomach twist with both sympathy and a strange sense of loss. He stepped away from the wheelhouse, moving toward her with a purposeful, almost predatory grace, and for a brief moment, she thought he might finally speak the words that had been hanging in the air between them. But he didn't.

"I can't do this," Kai said, his voice rough, the words lost in the wind. "I can't let you get dragged down into this."

Lila's heart sank as he took another step back, distancing himself from her. The intensity of his gaze shifted, his eyes shadowed with something unreadable, something raw. She knew he was holding back, holding on to something, but she didn't know what it was.

"Why?" she asked, her voice trembling with both frustration and something else—something she couldn't quite name. "Why won't you let me in? You've never let me in, Kai. I'm in this. I'm in this with you. With the sea. With the curse. And you can't keep pushing me away."

His jaw tightened, his hands curling into fists at his sides. "You don't understand," he muttered, his words a sharp growl. "This isn't something you can fix. This isn't something I can fix. The sea—it'll take us both. And there's nothing you can do to stop it."

Lila's chest tightened with the weight of his words. She had heard them before, but now they hit her differently, deeper. The truth that he had been trying to hide from her—the truth about the sea, about the curse, about their fates—was coming to a head, and there was no escaping it now. She could feel it, that cold, sinking feeling deep in her gut, as if the ocean itself were wrapping its tendrils around her heart, slowly pulling her under.

"You're wrong," she said, her voice steady, though her hands trembled as she gripped the railing tighter. "I can stop it. We can stop it. Together."

Kai's eyes darkened at her words, and for a moment, the air between them seemed to crackle with tension, like the calm before the storm. But then his expression softened, his shoulders slumping as though the weight of everything he had been holding back was too much to bear. He took a step toward her, his eyes searching hers with such intensity that it almost felt as if he were looking right through her, trying to find something that wasn't there.

"You don't understand," he whispered, his voice breaking. "You can't stop it. The curse… it's too powerful. And when the sea comes for us, it will take everything. Everyone. Me."

Lila's heart skipped a beat at his words, the implications of them crashing over her like the waves that battered the ship. She had always known, in the deepest part of herself, that this was bigger than just her or him. The sea had marked them both. But hearing it from his lips, hearing the fear in his voice, made everything feel so much more real, so much more terrifying.

"If we're both already marked," she said softly, her eyes searching his face for some sign of hope, some flicker of the man she had come to love, "then why fight it? Why not face it together? If the curse is inevitable, if the sea is going to take us, then let's take it on together. Let's face it together."

Kai's expression faltered, the hardness in his eyes warring with the raw emotion that flickered there. His hand reached out, brushing against her cheek with a tenderness that almost broke her. But even as he touched her, his eyes remained distant, as if he were still trying to protect her from something he couldn't even name.

"I can't lose you," he whispered, his voice so low she almost didn't hear it over the roar of the storm. "I can't lose you to this. I can't lose you to the sea."

Lila's breath caught in her throat at the weight of his words. The intensity of his gaze was like a flame burning through her chest, and she felt the pull of the ocean beneath her feet, its cold grip tightening around her heart. But even with the storm raging, even with the fury of the sea threatening to drown them both, she couldn't stop herself from leaning into him, pressing her lips against his in a kiss that was as desperate as it was tender.

The kiss was fierce, a meeting of hearts that had been broken and rebuilt in the shadow of the sea. It was a kiss filled with both longing and sorrow, as if they both knew the end was coming. As if they both knew that no matter what happened next, nothing would ever be the same. The storm howled around them, but in that moment, nothing else existed but the two of them, wrapped in the only thing they had left—the truth of their love.

When they finally pulled away, breathless and shaken, the storm seemed to pause, the wind dying down just enough for them to hear the world around them, the water slapping against the hull, the creak of the ship as it rocked in the aftermath of the storm.

"The sea is coming for us," Kai said, his voice barely a whisper, his forehead resting against hers. "And we can't stop it. But I won't let it take you. Not without a fight."

Lila's heart thundered in her chest at his words, the weight of them sinking in like a stone. But even as the fear threatened to overwhelm her, she felt something else—something deeper, something stronger. It wasn't just the sea that had marked them. It was their love, their bond, and no matter how dark the storm became, she wasn't going to let go.

"I'm not afraid," she whispered back, her voice steady despite the fear curling in her stomach. "I'm ready. And we'll fight it, Kai. Together."

He kissed her then, more gently this time, as if they both knew that whatever happened next, this was the last chance they had to claim something for themselves. The last chance to hold on to each other, to the love that had blossomed amidst the chaos of the sea.

And as the storm surged around them, as the tide began to rise, Lila knew that they had already given everything. They had given their hearts, their souls, to the sea. And no matter what happened next, no matter what the ocean took from them, they would face it together.

Because in the end, love was the only thing that could survive the storm.

And the final tide was rising.

www.ingramcontent.com/pod-product-compliance
Lightning Source LLC
LaVergne TN
LVHW020930200726
843506LV00011B/1906